THE QUEEN

RICHARD BRASSEY

GREAT-GREAT-GRANDPARENTS,
QUEEN VICTORIA
AND PRINCE ALBERT

GREAT-GRANDPARENTS,
KING EDWARD VII
AND QUEEN ALEXANDRA

GRANDPARENTS,
KING GEORGE V AND QUEEN MARY

MUM AND DAD,
THE DUKE AND DUCHE
OF YORK

First published in Great Britain in 2012
by Orion Children's Books
a division of the Orion Publishing Group Ltd
Orion House, 5 Upper St Martin's Lane, London WC2H 9EA
An Hachette UK Company

1 3 5 7 9 10 8 6 4 2

Text and illustrations copyright © Richard Brassey 2012

The right of Richard Brassey to be identified as
the author and illustrator of this work has been asserted.

A catalogue record for this book is available from the British Library

Printed in China

ISBN 978 1 4440 0127 3

www.orionbooks.co.uk

DAD'S OLDER BROTHER, UNCLE DAVID

GREAT-GREAT-UNCLE ARTHUR

GRANDDAD KING

GRANNY QUEEN

DAD

OTHER GRANDDAD

ARCHBISHOP

MUM

GODMOTHER AUNT MARY (MUM'S SISTER)

OTHER GRANNY

GODMOTHER AUNT MARY (DAD'S SISTER)

Princess Elizabeth was born in 1926. Her dad, Albert or 'Bertie', was the second son of King George V. At her christening she cried so much that she had to be given gripe water. It was the last time she ever cried in public. Her Great-Great-Uncle Arthur was one of her godfathers. Arthur's mum, Queen Victoria, had been born over a hundred years before in 1819.

When Elizabeth was less than a year old, her mum and dad went on a tour of Australia and New Zealand. She stayed with her grandparents, the King and Queen, and their pet parrot, Charlotte. The King nicknamed Elizabeth 'Lilibet'. It was six months before she saw her parents again. They returned with three tons of toys, which people had given as gifts for her.

For her fourth birthday, the King gave Lilibet a shetland pony named Peggy. A few months later Elizabeth's sister, Princess Margaret, was born. They had a nanny named Mrs Knight and a nursemaid named Miss MacDonald, who was known as 'Bobo'. Bobo was the only non-royal person allowed to call the Princess Lilibet. Sixty years later, long after Elizabeth became Queen, Bobo was still bringing her a cup of tea every morning.

The Duke and Duchess of York liked to call their family 'We four'. When they had time they all enjoyed nothing better than a pillow fight. Dad's older brother, Uncle David, often dropped by and joined in.

Every day Elizabeth and Margaret dressed alike. Sometimes they visited Mr J. M. Barrie. He was a very good storyteller. After all, he did write *Peter Pan*.

They spent their holidays visiting all the royal palaces with the King and Queen, and at Glamis Castle where their mum grew up. It's said to be the most haunted castle in Scotland.

GHOST IN ARMOUR

SECRET ROOMS

WHITE LADY

Y LADY

But their favourite house was 'The Little House', a child-sized cottage which was given to them by the people of Wales. When Elizabeth was eight, Dookie arrived. Dookie was her very first corgi.

His real name is *Rozavel Golden Eagle* but we call him Dookie.

Elizabeth and Margaret had a new governess, Miss Crawford, known as 'Crawfie'. They became very fond of her.

Ought we to play, Crawfie?

I cannot discharge my duties as King as I would wish to do without the help and support of the woman I love.

It's bad manners for royalty to smile in public.

UNCLE DAVID, BRIEFLY EDWARD VIII

When Elizabeth was ten, her granddad, the King, died. She was so sad, she thought she shouldn't play. Then Uncle David decided he didn't want to be King because it meant he couldn't marry his divorced girlfriend. In those days a divorced person wasn't allowed to marry the monarch.

So her dad, the next oldest son of George V, became King George VI. He used his last name, George, although the family still called him Bertie. The next thing, they'd moved into Buckingham Palace and were waving from the balcony. The royals often wave from the balcony on great occasions.

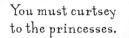

You must curtsey to the princesses.

If you want it, you have to carry it yourself.

Although she was now heir to the throne, Elizabeth's mum and dad wanted her to do things other girls did. A group of Girl Guides was formed which met in the gardens of Buckingham Palace. The other girls were expected to curtsey to Elizabeth. Margaret became a Brownie.

One day the princesses went to tea with Crawfie, at the YWCA in Tottenham Court Road. They even travelled on the underground. Elizabeth did not expect to have to carry her own teapot to the table. They'd hoped not to be recognised, but a crowd gathered to stare.

When the Second World War broke out, Elizabeth and Margaret were sent to live at Windsor Castle, which was safer from bombs than London. Elizabeth had lessons all by herself with an absent-minded schoolmaster from a nearby boys' school. Sometimes he quite forgot he wasn't in a class full of boys.

At eighteen Elizabeth joined the women's army. She learnt how to change the tyre on a truck. The other girls slept in huts but she went home each night to the castle. Then the war ended and it was back to Buckingham Palace and the balcony, with Prime Minister Winston Churchill, to celebrate. A few years earlier she'd met a prince from Greece called Philip. Soon his photo appeared on her desk.

The King and Queen liked Philip and said that he and Elizabeth could get married. Two nights before the wedding a big party was held at Buckingham Palace. The King led the guests in such a merry conga that the Queen of the Netherlands' tiara fell off. After the wedding ceremony it was back to the balcony. A year later, Prince Charles was born. Princess Anne came along two years after that.

The King had become ill. He died while Elizabeth and Philip were on safari in the bright sunshine of Kenya, staying at the Treetops Hotel. Elizabeth was now Queen.

She hurried home. The young Queen was met at Heathrow Airport by her elderly Prime Minister, Winston Churchill. It was a gloomy winter's day.

On the morning of her coronation, Elizabeth and Philip left Buckingham Palace in the antique, gold state coach for the ride to Westminster Abbey.

It was a drizzly day. Among other kings and queens in the procession, Queen Salote of Tonga ignored the rain and waved cheerily from an open carriage.

The Abbey was stuffed full of lords and ladies in their robes. Elizabeth sat on the same throne which had first been used, by King Edward I, 650 years before. The Archbishop of Canterbury placed the crown upon her head and trumpets sounded.

GOD SAVE THE QUEEN!

A few months later, Charles and Anne were left at home while the new Queen and Philip set off to tour the Commonwealth. They visited Bermuda, the Bahamas, Jamaica and Belize. Sometimes Elizabeth looked grumpy. It was hard to keep smiling in the bright sun. Then to Fiji and to Tonga, where Queen Salote entertained them. In New Zealand the Maoris welcomed Her Majesty with a haka.

In Sri Lanka the royal couple saw the Perahera, a religious festival with 125 exotically-robed elephants. Finally they started for home. In Libya, the spanking-new royal yacht *Britannia* met them from England with Charles and Anne on board. They hadn't seen each other for six months. For the next forty-four years *HMY Britannia* would be Her Majesty's floating palace.

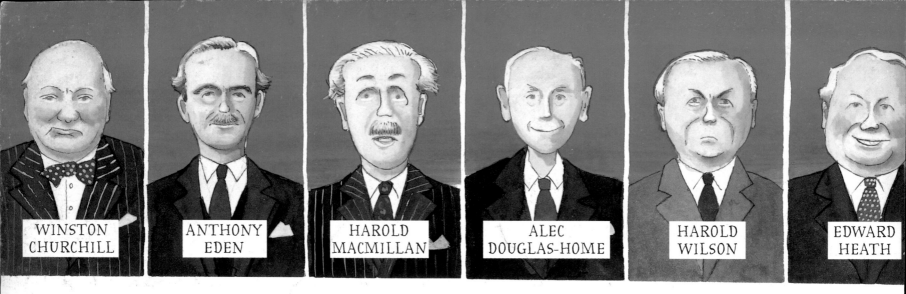

WINSTON CHURCHILL · **ANTHONY EDEN** · **HAROLD MACMILLAN** · **ALEC DOUGLAS-HOME** · **HAROLD WILSON** · **EDWARD HEATH**

Queen Elizabeth has seen twelve prime ministers come and go during her reign. She'll probably see quite a few more. Her first, Winston Churchill, was fifty-two years older than her; David Cameron is forty years younger. She meets her PM once a week and tells him what she thinks about the way he's running the country, but he doesn't have to take her advice.

JAMES CALLAGHAN · **MARGARET THATCHER** · **JOHN MAJOR** · **TONY BLAIR** · **GORDON BROWN** · **DAVID CAMERON**

PRINCE CHARLES

CAMILLA

DIANA

PRINCESS ANNE

PRINCE ANDREW

PRINCE EDWARD

She has four children – Charles, Anne, Andrew and Edward – eight grandchildren and one great grandchild. Charles, the Prince of Wales, is heir to the throne. His son, William, is next in line. He is the son of Charles' first wife, Diana, who died in a car crash. Charles' second wife is Camilla. William is married to Catherine, known as Kate. The Queen has had as many as eleven corgis at any one time.

PRINCE WILLIAM

KATE

THE QUEEN AND HER GRANDCHILDREN

The Queen's main house is Buckingham Palace. Here she knights people, presents them with medals, holds enormous garden parties in the summer, gives lavish dinners for visiting heads of state, and waves from the balcony.

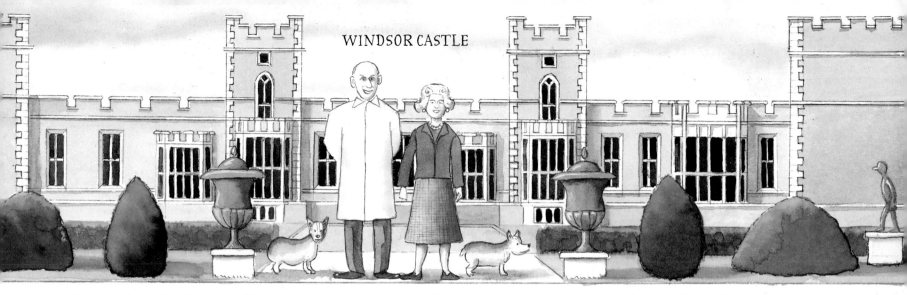

At the weekends she usually goes to Windsor Castle. Summer is spent at Balmoral Castle in Scotland and Christmas at Sandringham in Norfolk. The Christmas decorations are never taken down until she leaves in February. The Queen is happiest in the countryside, especially in Scotland.

HORSE RACING

THE QUEEN LIKES

CORGIS

AFTERNOON TEA

HER COMMONWEALTH

The Queen's great-grandfather, Edward VII, liked holding his birthday party in summer and every monarch since has had two birthdays – a real one, and an official one in June with Trooping the Colour and a balcony appearance. She is already the oldest British monarch ever. 2012 will mark her Diamond Jubilee – sixty years on the throne. In 2015 she'll overtake Queen Victoria to become the longest reigning British monarch, although she still has a way to go before beating the world record.

QUEEN VICTORIA
63 YEARS

KING BHUMIBOL
OF THAILAND
LONGEST REIGNING
LIVING KING

LOUIS XIV OF FRANCE
72 YEARS

PEPI II OF ANCIENT
EGYPT MAY HAVE
REIGNED 94 YEARS
THE LONGEST EVER